D1101382

My First EASTER Book

WITHDRAWN FROM STOCK

Jane Winstanley

W

FRANKLIN WATTS

LONDON • SYDNEY

Franklin Watts
First published in Great Britain in 2015 by
The Watts Publishing Group

Copyright © The Watts Publishing Group 2015

All rights reserved.

Credits

Editor: Nicola Barber
Design: Storeybooks
Picture Research: Diana Morris
Illustrator: Shelagh McNicholas, pp 6–9
Cover design: Cathyrn Gilbert
Extra artwork by Ruth Walton
Commissioned photography:
  Paul Bricknell Photography p12, 13t, 15m, 21b,
  25b, 29m, 32
  Tudor Photography, Banbury pp18–19, 20–21,
  24–25, 26–27, 28–29, 31t

Every attempt has been made to clear copyright.
Should there be any inadvertent omission please
apply to the publisher for rectification.

Dewey number 394.2'667
HB ISBN 978 1 4451 3974 6
Library ebook ISBN 978 1 4451 3975 3

Printed in China

FSC
www.fsc.org

MIX
Paper from
responsible sources
FSC® C104740

Franklin Watts
An imprint of Hachette Children's Group
Part of The Watts Publishing Group
Carmelite House
50 Victoria Embankment
London EC4Y 0DZ

An Hachette UK Company
www.hachette.co.uk

www.franklinwatts.co.uk

Picture credits:

Borders and backgrounds; 3, 4, 10, 17,22;
Shutterstock/Kalenik Hanna; 12, 13, 18, 19, 20,
21, 24, 25, 26, 27, 28, 29; Dmitry Kalinovsky/
Shutterstock 2b & 31; Jorisvo/Shutterstock 4m;
Markova/Shutterstock 4b; Elizabeth Hoffmann/
Dreamstime.com 5tr; ValeStock/Shutterstock.com 5tl;
Shiningcolors/Dreamstime.com 5b; Alan Suddaby/
Buttonsoup 10tm; Vnlit/Dreamstime.com 10tl; JackK/
Shutterstock 10tr; Agfoto/Shutterstock 10bl; Douglas
Freer/Shutterstock 10br; Cvalie/Shutterstock 11t;
Edward Marques-mortimer/Dreamstime.com 11m;
Wendy Kaveney Photography/Shutterstock.com 11b;
Douglas Freer/Shutterstock 13m; Brulove/Shutterstock
13b; Snake8/Dreamstime.com 14t; Richard Gunion/
Dreamstime.com 14b; Protasov AN/Shutterstock 15t;
Edward Westmacott/Shutterstock 15b & 30; Christian
Vince/Shutterstock 16l; George P. Choma/Shutterstock
16r; Barbara Delgado-millea/Dreamstime.com
17t; Alexander Makarov/Dreamstime.com 19b;
Jenkedco/Shutterstock 22; Lev Radin/Shutterstock 23t
& m; Tatiana Sayig/Shutterstock 23b; Africa Studio/
Shutterstock 25b; Irina Fischer/Shutterstock 27b; Lakov
Filimonov/Shutterstock 29b.

Contents

What is Easter?   4

The Easter story   6

Shrove Tuesday   10

How to make pancakes   12

All about Lent   14

Easter Sunday   16

How to decorate Easter eggs   18

Make an Easter flower garden   20

Easter parades   22

Make an Easter chick card   24

Make Easter egg nests   26

Make a rabbit-ears hat   28

Glossary   30

Index   32

Words in **bold** are in the glossary on page 30.

What is Easter?

Easter is celebrated every year by millions of people all over the world. But what is Easter and why do we celebrate it?

The first Easter

Easter is the most important time in the **Christian** year. The day that Jesus was put to death on a cross is called **Good Friday**. Christians believe that Jesus came back to life again two days later. This was the first Easter. It is celebrated on Easter Sunday.

Pre-Christian celebrations

In the **northern hemisphere**, Easter usually falls at the beginning of spring. But long before Jesus Christ, people celebrated the arrival of spring after the cold, dark days of winter. Many Easter traditions come from these ancient springtime festivals.

People celebrate Easter in different ways around the world. What do you enjoy the most at Easter?

Eating chocolate eggs?

Hunting for Easter eggs?

Wearing Easter bonnets?

The Easter story

Jesus had been spreading God's word in towns and villages all over **Palestine**. Many people loved him but others did not like him, or the words he spoke.

Jesus and his twelve **disciples** went to Jerusalem for the Jewish feast of **Passover**. Jesus had many enemies in Jerusalem. He knew they would kill him. On the way Jesus warned his disciples that he would soon die.

Some people believed that God would one day send a new King of the Jews. They said he would enter Jerusalem on a donkey.

Jesus borrowed a donkey and rode on it into Jerusalem. The crowds shouted "Jesus is King!" They threw **palm** leaves down in front of Jesus.

Some of the **priests** were unhappy that Jesus was so popular. They offered Judas, one of the disciples, thirty pieces of silver to betray his friend. Judas took the money.

Later that week Jesus and his twelve disciples sat down for a meal together. Jesus told them that one of the disciples had already taken money to betray him. He explained that he would be **arrested** and killed. But he told the disciples not to be sad because he was going to **heaven** to be with God.

That night Jesus went with some of the disciples to the Garden of Gethsemane to pray. In the early morning, Judas arrived with guards and soldiers. The guards arrested Jesus and took him to Pontius Pilate, the Roman leader. He was tried and sentenced to death.

Jesus was given a crown of sharp thorns to wear on his head. He was made to drag a large wooden cross to the top of a nearby hill. The soldiers nailed Jesus to the cross and raised it up with a sign saying, 'The King of the Jews'.

That night Jesus died. Jesus's friends took his body and laid it in a **tomb**. They rolled a heavy stone across the entrance to seal the tomb.

This stone tomb is like the one that Jesus was laid in on the night he died.

Two days later a friend of Jesus called Mary Magdalen went to visit the tomb. When she got there she found that the stone had been rolled away from the entrance. Inside there was no sign of Jesus's body.

As Mary stood alone, crying, Jesus appeared before her and spoke to her. Mary told the disciples what had happened, but at first they did not believe her.

Then Jesus appeared to the disciples. He told them. "Go into the world, and preach the **gospel** to everyone." Later, Jesus went up to heaven to be with God.

Shrove Tuesday

Shrove Tuesday is the day before **Lent.** Lent is the important run up to Easter (see pages 14–15). In the past, many people did not eat meat, eggs, sugar and butter during Lent. Today, some people give up treats like chocolate instead.

Shrove Tuesday was the day when people held feasts to use up all the food they were not going to eat during Lent.

These are some of the delicious treats people still make on Shrove Tuesday.

Poland – paczki doughnuts fried in oil

Australia – thick pancakes served cold with cream and jam

Canada – pancakes served with sausages and jam

Great Britain – pancakes served with lemon and sugar

Sweden – round buns filled with marzipan and thick cream

Celebrations

In many parts of the world there are spectacular celebrations on Shrove Tuesday.

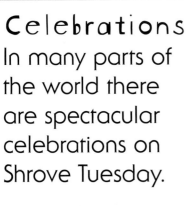

In Venice, Italy, people wear crazy carnival masks. There are parades and street theatre performances.

In some places Shrove Tuesday is called **Mardi Gras**. In cities such as New Orleans, in the USA, and Rio de Janeiro, in Brazil there are big Mardi Gras parades. Millions of people go to watch the decorated **floats**, to dance and have fun.

How to make pancakes

S hrove Tuesday is sometimes called 'pancake day'. In the past people made pancakes to use up all their eggs, sugar and butter before Lent. Pancakes are made in a very hot pan, so ask an adult to cook them for you.

You will need:
* bowl, whisk and cup
* 110g plain flour
* pinch of salt
* 1 egg
* 275ml milk
* frying pan and fish slice
* butter for frying
* plate
! Hot fat is very dangerous – ask a grown-up to help

Instructions

1 Sift the flour and salt into a bowl.

2 Crack the egg into a cup. Make a hole in the centre of the flour and pour in the egg.

3 Add a little of the milk and mix well with a hand whisk. Add the rest of the milk gradually, whisking all the time.

Ask an adult to do steps 4–7 while you prepare the fillings.

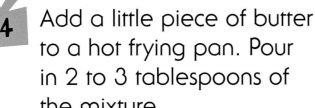

4 Add a little piece of butter to a hot frying pan. Pour in 2 to 3 tablespoons of the mixture.

5 Swirl the pan round gently so that the base of the pan is coated with the mixture. Leave for 2 to 3 minutes until it is almost set.

6 Flip the pancake over with a fish slice. Cook for a further 2 to 3 minutes.

7 Slide the pancake out on to a plate.

Pancake fillings

Pancakes are tasty served simply with a squeeze of lemon juice and a sprinkle of sugar. But there are lots of other ways to enjoy pancakes. Try these yummy fillings:

* raspberries and ice cream with a drizzle of raspberry sauce

* sliced banana and ice cream

* banana and maple syrup

All about Lent

The time leading up to Easter is called Lent.

Forty days

The traditions of Lent come from the forty days that Jesus spent in the desert, praying and preparing to do God's work. During that time he did not eat. Some people try to follow his example and give up treats during the forty days of Lent.

Ash Wednesday

The first day of Lent is called **Ash Wednesday**. In some churches, the priest makes the mark of a cross on each person's forehead with ash. The ash comes from burned **palm crosses** from the previous year. The ash crosses are signs that people are sorry for things they have done wrong in the past year.

Palm Sunday

The last week of Lent, leading up to Easter, is called **Holy Week**. It starts with **Palm Sunday**. On this day, Christians carry a cross made from the leaves of a palm tree. The cross celebrates Jesus's arrival in Jerusalem on a donkey, when the crowds laid down palm leaves in front of him.

Good Friday

On Good Friday, Christians all over the world remember Jesus's death on the cross. Many people go to church services to reflect on the **crucifixion**.

It is traditional to eat hot cross buns on Good Friday. These are spicy buns with a pastry cross on the top. The buns remind people of the cross on which Jesus was crucified.

Easter Sunday

Easter Sunday is one of the two most important days for Christians (the other is Christmas Day). Easter Sunday is a very happy day when they remember that Jesus came back from the dead (the **resurrection**). Christians all over the world attend special church services.

Sunrise service

Some Christians take part in a sunrise service early on Easter Sunday. They gather together outside to watch the sun come up as a symbol of hope for the future.

Easter Sunday is a holiday in many countries. People give each other cards and gifts of eggs. In many parts of the world, Easter eggs are made out of chocolate. In some countries they are beautifully decorated hens' eggs.

Easter egg hunts are a popular tradition on Easter Sunday. In towns and villages in Europe, Australia and the USA, the Easter bunny hides eggs for children to find.

How to decorate Easter eggs

You can give these colourful eggs as Easter gifts, or arrange them in a basket as pretty Easter decorations.

You will need:
* newspaper
* kitchen paper
* 3 teaspoons white vinegar
* food colourings
* eggs (either hard-boiled or blown) and egg box
* rubber bands
* 250ml water

Instructions

1. Cover a work surface in thick newspaper. Place the kitchen paper on top of the newspaper.

   Pour the vinegar on to the kitchen paper. Drip on some food colouring.

2. Fold the kitchen paper around an egg. Put the rubber bands around the paper to hold it in place. Pour on some water.

3. Repeat steps 1 and 2 with more kitchen paper and eggs.

4 Put the eggs in the egg box to dry overnight.

 5 Take off the paper to reveal the pattern.

Fabergé eggs

In 1885, the Russian emperor asked a Russian jeweller called Peter Carl Fabergé to design a jewel-encrusted egg as an Easter present for his wife. The empress was delighted, and the tradition continued almost every Easter until 1917. Each valuable Fabergé egg is different, but they all open to reveal a secret – some have moving parts, others contain tiny paintings, sculptures, clocks or miniature ships.

Make an Easter flower garden

In some parts of the world many colourful spring flowers come into bloom around Easter time. This garden of flowers will last a lot longer than real ones.

You will need:
* egg box
* coloured paints/felt-tip pens
* coloured paper
* pencil
* scissors
* glue and spreader
* lolly sticks
* bottle caps
* modelling clay
* chick decoration

Instructions

Paint the egg box green – leave it to dry.

Daffodils

1 Draw a daffodil flower on a piece of yellow paper and cut it out. Draw round the shape on a second piece of paper and cut it out.

2 Glue the two pieces of paper together with a lolly stick sandwiched between them.

3 Paint the bottle cap yellow and leave it to dry. Glue the bottle cap in the centre of the flower. Glue long green petals cut from green paper to the lolly stick.

Tulips

1. Draw a tulip flower on a piece of coloured paper and cut it out. Draw round the shape on a second piece of paper and cut it out.

2. Glue the two pieces of paper together with the lolly stick sandwiched between them. Decorate the tulip with a funky pattern.

3. Glue long green leaves cut from green paper to the lolly stick.

Put some modelling clay into the bottom of the egg box. Push the lolly sticks into the modelling clay to make a colourful garden of spring flowers. Add a chick decoration as shown in the picture below.

21

Easter parades

Easter parades are held all over the world. Some are Christian festivals. Others are now just for fun.

There are Easter Day parades in cities all over the USA. The Fifth Avenue parade in New York is the most famous. People wear their best clothes and beautifully decorated hats.

This float shows Jesus after his resurrection. It is part of a religious Easter day parade in Central America.

In the past, people wore plain, dull clothes during Lent. Then, once Lent was over they decorated their hats with flowers to go to church. Today, people still wear 'Easter bonnets' on Easter Sunday.

Make an Easter chick card

Wish someone a 'Happy Easter' with this card. It opens up to reveal a chick.

You will need:
* A4-sized thin white card x 2
* scissors
* coloured felt-tip pens
* thin yellow card
* glue and spreader
* scrap of orange card
* split pin

Instructions

1 Carefully fold an A4 piece of thin card in half.

2 Cut out an egg shape from another piece of thin card. Make sure the shape will fit on the front of the card. Decorate it on one side.

3 Turn the egg shape over. Cut it in half across the middle with a zig-zag line.

4 Draw the body and head of an Easter chick on the yellow card. Cut it out.

24

5 Spread glue on to the back of the chick. Glue the chick on to the card. Draw on two eyes.

Cut a beak shape from the orange card. Glue it on to the head of the chick.

 6 Glue the bottom half of the egg over the chick.

 7 Ask an adult to fix the top of the egg on to the card with the split pin as shown.

Easter chicks

Chicks hatching are a sign of new life. Easter cards are sometimes decorated with chicks to remind people of Jesus's resurrection.

Make Easter egg nests

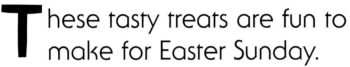

These tasty treats are fun to make for Easter Sunday.

You will need:
* 100g chocolate
* 50g butter
* 2 tablespoons golden syrup
* 75g cornflakes
* microwave-proof bowl
* wooden spoon and teaspoon
* cake cases
* mini eggs and chicks

Instructions

1 Break the chocolate into pieces and put them in a bowl with the butter and golden syrup.

2 Ask an adult to melt the mixture in the microwave for 30 seconds. Or get help to melt it in a bowl over a pan of boiling water.

3 Add the cornflakes to the chocolate mixture, being careful not to crush them too much.

4 When the cornflakes are all coated with chocolate, spoon some of the mixture into each cake case.

Make a hollow in the middle with the back of a spoon.

 5 Put the egg nests in the fridge to set.

Decorate with mini eggs and chicks.

Easter eggs

In the past, people did not eat eggs during Lent, so there were lots to use up at Easter time. Cracking open an egg reminds Christians of the empty tomb and Jesus's resurrection from the dead.

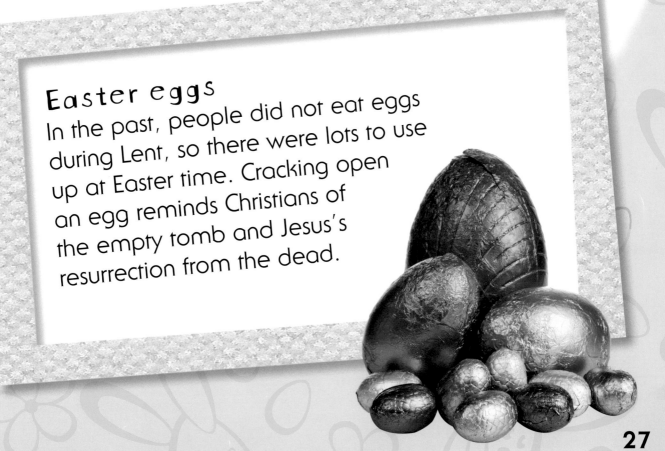

Make a rabbit- ears hat

T ry making this fun rabbit- ears hat for Easter.

You will need:
* thin white card
* ruler
* pencil
* scissors
* sticky tape
* pink paper
* glue and spreader
* cotton wool

Instructions

1. Cut a strip of white card about 5cm wide. It needs to be long enough to wrap around your head and overlap by about 2cm. Use sticky tape to join the band so that it fits comfortably around your head.

2. Cut two ears out of white card each about 20cm long x 8cm wide. Cut two smaller ears out of pink paper.

3. Cover the white ears in glue and stick cotton wool on.

28

4 Glue the pink ears on to the centre of each cotton-wool-covered ear.

5 Glue the ears inside the band on either side of the join.

The Easter bunny
Rabbits have lots of babies. They are seen as a symbol of new life.

In some countries, the Easter bunny leaves a basket of chocolate eggs and other treats for children on Easter Sunday morning.

Glossary

arrest To seize someone by law.

Ash Wednesday The first day of Lent. It gets its name from the ashes used to make the mark of a cross on a person's forehead.

Christian A person who follows the teachings of Jesus Christ.

crucifixion An ancient method of execution. The victim was nailed or bound to a cross shape made from wood and left to die.

disciple A follower of Christ.

float In a parade or carnival, a float is a decorated platform mounted on a truck that moves slowly along the streets.

Good Friday The Friday of Holy Week when Christians believe Jesus was crucified and died.

gospel The teaching of Jesus Christ.

heaven In Christianity, the home of God, of the angels and of the good after death.

Holy Week The week leading up to Easter Sunday, which starts with Palm Sunday.

Lent The forty days before Easter, starting with Ash Wednesday.

Mardi Gras Another term for Shrove

Tuesday – in French it means 'Fat Tuesday' because it was the day that people used up all the fats and other foods they were not allowed to eat during Lent.

northern hemisphere The northern half of the Earth's surface, north of the Equator.

Palestine In Bible times, Palestine was a region on the eastern shore of the Mediterranean Sea.

palm A tree that has a crown of long, feathered leaves.

palm cross A cross made from palm leaves.

Palm Sunday The Sunday before Easter, when Jesus entered Jerusalem on a donkey.

Passover A Jewish festival that remembers the time when the Israelites (Jews) escaped from Egyptian slavery.

priest A person who carries out the sacred rites of a religion.

resurrection In Christianity, the belief that Jesus Christ rose from the dead on Easter Sunday.

Shrove Tuesday The day before Ash Wednesday.

tomb A place, often underground, for burying the dead.

Index

Ash Wednesday 14

chicks 24–25, 26, 27
chocolate 5, 10, 16,
      26–27, 29
Christmas day 16
crucifixion 4, 8, 15

disciples 6, 7
donkeys 6

Easter bonnets 5, 23
Easter bunny 17, 29
Easter cards 16, 24–25
Easter eggs 5, 16, 17,
      18–19, 26–27, 29
Easter story 6–9
Easter Sunday 4, 16–17,
      22, 23, 29
egg hunts 5, 17

Fabergé eggs 19
Fabergé, Peter Carl 19
floats 11, 22
flowers 20–21
forty days 14

Garden of Gethsemane 7
Good Friday 4, 15

Holy Week 15
hot cross buns 15

Jerusalem 6, 15
Jesus Christ 4, 6–9, 14,
      15, 16, 22, 25, 27
Judas 6, 7

Lent 10, 12, 14–15,
      23, 27

Mardis Gras 11
Mary Magdalen 9
masks 11

paczki doughnuts 10
palm crosses 14, 15
palm leaves 6, 14, 15
Palm Sunday 15
pancakes 10, 12–13
parades 11, 22–23
Passover 6
Pontius Pilate 7
pre-Christian festivals 4

rabbits 28–29
resurrection 9, 16, 22,
      25, 27

Shrove Tuesday 10–11,
      12
spring 4, 20–21

tombs 8, 9, 27

Olympic Sports

Nick Hunter

WAYLAND

First published in 2011 by Wayland

Copyright © Wayland 2011

Wayland
338 Euston Road
London NW1 3BH

Wayland Australia
Level 17/207 Kent Street
Sydney, NSW 2000

All rights reserved

Produced for Wayland by Calcium
Design: Simon Borrough and Paul Myerscough
Editor: Sarah Eason
Editor for Wayland: Katie Woolley
Picture researcher: Susannah Jayes

British Library Cataloguing in Publication Data

Hunter, Nick.
   Olympic sports.—(The Olympics)
   1. Olympic Games (30th : 2012 : London, England)—
   Juvenile literature. 2. Sports—Juvenile literature.
   I. Title II. Series
   796.4'8-dc22

ISBN: 978 0 7502 6436 5

Printed in China
Wayland is a division of Hachette Children's Books,
an Hachette UK company.
www.hachette.co.uk

The website addresses (URLs) included in this book were
valid at the time of going to press. However, because
of the nature of the internet, it is possible that some
addresses may have changed, or sites may have changed
or closed down since publication. While the author and
Publisher regret any inconvenience this may cause the
readers, no responsibility for any such changes can be
accepted by either the author or the Publisher.

Picture Acknowledgements:

Cover Main image: Shutterstock: Jamie Roach. Inset
images: Shutterstock: John Lumb tl, Muzsy tr, Chad
McDermott bl, Pete Niesen br. Spine image:
Shutterstock: Herbert Kratky. Back cover image:
Shutterstock: Peter Kirillov.
Pages Corbis: Jens Buettner/EPA 13b, Fabrice Coffrini/
EPA 6, Kimimasa Mayama/Reuters 14, Reix-Liewig/For
Pictures 4, Zhang Chen/xh/Xinhua Press 25tr; Dreamstime:
Bedo 23tl, Fstockfoto 21br, Pniesen 7, Nadiya Vlashchenko
28; Getty Images: 18, AFP 9, 17, 20; London 2012: 5,
28-29; PA Photos: 23br; Shutterstock: Galina Barskaya
15tr, Olga Besnard 24, Vince Clements 19, Chris Curtis
10, Adam Fraise 21tr, Fstockfoto 11tr, 22, 25bl, 26, 27,
Herbert Kratky 1, PhotoStock10 15bl, Chen Wei Seng
29, Sportgraphic 11bl, 13tr, Sportsphotographer.eu 8,
Webitect 2, 16, Vladimir Wrangel 12.

ROTHERHAM LIBRARY &
INFORMATION SERVICES
JNF
OES 462293
B52 003 3071
SCHOOLS STOCK

Contents

The world watches   **4**

On your marks   **6**

Jumping and throwing   **8**

All-round athletes   **10**

Endurance athletes   **12**

Gymnastics   **14**

In the pool   **16**

On the water   **18**

Combat sports   **20**

Team sports   **22**

What a racket!   **24**

Winter sports   **26**

Changing Olympic sports   **28**

Olympic trivia   **30**

Glossary   **31**

Further information and Index   **32**

The world watches

It is late July 2012. At different **venues** across London and the rest of the United Kingdom, spectators are watching as some of the world's greatest athletes take the stage. At the Velodrome, track cyclists are racing wheel to wheel. In the table tennis arena, fans are amazed by the players' lightning-fast reflexes. Cheering crowds applaud the performances, from the athletes in the Olympic Stadium to the beach volleyball players at Horse Guards Parade.

Jamaican sprinter Usain Bolt took the gold medal in the men's 200-metre race at the 2008 Games in Beijing, and he is a hot favourite to win again in 2012.

Olympic insights

Some unusual events have been part of the Olympics throughout history. In 1904, the 'plunge for distance' was part of the St Louis Olympics. Competitors dived into a pool and stayed motionless. The athlete who dived the furthest and remained under water the longest was the winner.

The Olympic story

Olympic history goes back thousands of years to ancient Greece, where the first Games were held in 776 BCE. The first Olympics included only a single running race, but it wasn't long before other sports were added. The Games died out with the ancient Greeks in 349 CE, but were brought to life once more in 1896, when the first 'modern' Olympic Games were held in Athens, Greece. Then it was decided that, as well as the Summer Olympics, a Winter Olympics for snow and ice sports would be held. It was first staged in 1924 in Chamonix, France. Then, in 1960 in Rome, Italy, the first **Paralympics** for athletes with disabilities took place.

London's turn

Today, the Summer Olympics are held every four years by a **host** country. The Winter Olympics take place two years after the Summer Olympics. In 2012, the world will look to London, the next Summer Olympic host city. There, people will see a wide range of sports – some can trace their **origins** back to the ancient Games, but there are plenty of exciting 'modern-day' sports too, including BMX racing, basketball, shooting and sailing.

Olympics by numbers

There will be **26** different sports at the London Olympics in 2012 and **300** separate events. Athletics awards gold medals in **47** events and swimming has **34** different events.

In 2012, London will put on the greatest sporting show on Earth. Many events will take place in the Olympic Stadium.

On your marks

For many spectators, events on the athletics track in the Olympic Stadium are what the Games are all about. Whether they are sprinting or running long distance races, all track athletes need stamina, speed, strength and clear tactics to win.

What makes a great sprinter?

Sprint races are all about power and pace as races are often decided by fractions of a second. A fast start is essential and by pushing off starting blocks, runners can get away quickly. New materials have made it possible to create lighter running shoes and rubberised race tracks that can stop runners slipping – helping them gain those extra few hundredths of a second. Sprint **hurdlers** must also combine the pace of a sprinter with great jumping techniques to clear 10 hurdles during the race.

Olympic insights

A runner has finished when his or her torso, from shoulder to waist, crosses the finish line. In a close race, sprinters lean forwards, or dip, at the finish to get a little extra advantage.

In the 100-metre race at the Athens Games in 2004, US sprinter Justin Gatlin (right) crossed the line first to take the gold medal. Portugal's Francis Obikwelu (second from left) dipped to take the silver.

Tactical racing

Track races are not just for sprinters. Races are also run at 400, 800, 1,500, 5,000 and 10,000 metres. The 3,000-metre **steeplechase** includes hurdles and a jump over water.

Many of the most amazing Olympic performances have been in long-distance competitions, in which African athletes have dominated recent Olympics. Ethiopian greats, Tirunesh Dibaba (female) and Kenenisa Bekele (male) won two gold medals each at the 5,000- and 10,000-metre races in Beijing.

Kenyan Brimin Kipruto (centre) took the gold medal in the 3,000-metre steeplechase at the 2008 Games in Beijing.

Olympics by numbers
Here are some of the greatest athletics wins:
100 metres – Women
Florence Griffith-Joyner (USA), **10.62** *seconds (1988)*
400 metres – Men
Michael Johnson (USA), **43.49** *seconds (1996)*
400 metres – Women
Marie-José Pérec (France), **48.25** *seconds (1996)*
1,500 metres – Men
Noah Ngeny (Kenya), **3** *minutes,* **32.07** *seconds (2000)*
10,000 metres – Men
Kenenisa Bekele (Ethiopia), **27** *minutes,* **01.17** *seconds (2008)*
100 metres – Men
Usain Bolt (Jamaica), **9.69** *seconds (2008)*
10,000 metres – Women
Tirunesh Dibaba (Ethiopia), **29** *minutes,* **54.66** *seconds (2008)*

> When anyone tells me I can't do anything, I'm just not listening anymore.
> Florence Griffith-Joyner, 1988 100-metre sprint gold medallist.

Jumping and throwing

Athletics also features field events, including long jump, triple jump, high jump and throwing contests, such as **shot put**, **javelin** and **discus**. The Olympic motto is 'Faster, Higher, Stronger' and athletes must be all three to triumph in field events.

The high jump technique of leaping backwards over the pole is called the 'Fosbury Flop'. It is named after Dick Fosbury of the USA, who first performed the move at the 1968 Olympics, where he took the gold medal.

Leaping for gold

In high jump and pole vault, athletes must clear a horizontal bar without touching it. High jumpers leap backwards over the bar to land on their backs. Pole vaulters use a long pole to propel themselves high into the air and over the bar. They must have great upper body strength and agility to jump heights of more than five metres. In long jump and triple jump, athletes take a run-up before jumping as far as possible into a sand pit.

Strength and technique

Olympic throwing events include the **hammer**, shot put, discus and javelin competitions. While each sport requires upper body strength, technique is just as important. Hammer and discus athletes spin around to give their throws added force. Athletes must aim precisely and release the ball at exactly the right moment to ensure a successful throw.

Olympics by numbers

Event	What is thrown?
shot put	metal ball weighing **7.26** kilograms (men) and **4** kilograms (women)
discus	metal disc weighing **2** kilograms (men) and **1** kilogram (women)
hammer	metal ball attached to a metal cable and handle, weighing **7.26** kilograms (men) and **4** kilograms (women)
javelin	**2.6** to **2.7** metres long and weighing **800** grams (men), **2.2** to **2.3** metres long and weighing **600** grams (women)

The shot put competition has been an Olympic event since its first appearance at the 1912 Games.

Olympic insights

Javelin and discus throwing were both part of the ancient Olympic Games. Like many ancient Olympic sports, javelin throwing was part of the training for ancient Greek soldiers. The hammer throw has its origins in **sledgehammer** throwing in sixteenth century Scotland and England.

9

All-round athletes

Some of the toughest competitors at the Olympics are all-round athletes who take part in events such as the triathlon, decathlon and heptathlon. These challenging competitions require participants to complete several gruelling events, in which they must demonstrate athletic skills including running, jumping, cycling and throwing.

Road cycling is one of three categories that make up the triathlon event. The other categories are swimming and running.

Olympic insights

Only a few athletes have won medals at both Summer and Winter Olympics. Edward Eagan (USA) won gold in both boxing (1920 Summer Olympics) and **bobsleigh** (1932 Winter Olympics). More recently, Canada's Clara Hughes won two bronze medals in cycling in 1996 and has won four speed skating medals at three Winter Olympics in 2002, 2006 and 2010.

Ancient all-rounders

All-round athletes were revered at the ancient Olympics in Greece. The greatest Olympic champion was the winner of the pentathlon, which included a running race, discus and javelin throws, long jump and wrestling. Today, the 'modern' pentathlon includes different sports such as fencing and shooting. The triathlon was introduced to the Olympics in 2000 and in 2012, the triathlon will be held in London's Hyde Park, with the swimming stage taking place in the park's Serpentine Lake.

The 'modern' pentathlon includes five events: fencing (above), horse riding, running, swimming and shooting.

Long jumpers extend their legs and push their torso forwards to gain the maximum distance in their jump.

WORD FILE

decathlon event (men): features ten sports over two days. A 100-metre sprint, long jump, shot put, high jump and 400-metre race make up day one. Day two includes 110-metre hurdles, discus, pole vault, javelin and the final 1,500-metre race

heptathlon event (women): features seven sports over two days. Day one includes 100-metre hurdles, high jump, shot put and a 200-metre sprint. Day two sports are long jump, javelin and the 800-metre race

Endurance athletes

Many sports test athletes' stamina, from rowing and road cycling to the marathon and the 10-kilometre swim. To be successful, athletes in endurance events must be able to maintain high energy levels over long periods of time by eating a high-energy diet and improving their stamina through training. On average, endurance athletes spend six hours a day training to achieve the fitness levels required to compete in an Olympic event.

Rowing uses more muscle groups than almost any other sport as the athletes push themselves to 40 or 45 oar strokes per minute.

WORD FILE

Key rowing terms and their meanings:

bow: *front section of a boat or shell*

coxswain or cox: *person who sits at the stern of the boat during some rowing races to steer and direct the rowers*

full paddle: *rowing as fast as possible*

sculls: *rowing with two oars per person. Sculls events can include one, two or four people*

shell: *rowing boat for racing, made of wood or **carbon fibre***

sweep: *rowing with one oar. Sweep rowers race in teams of two, four or eight*

Longest Olympic races

Cycling road races are long, tactical battles. The men's road race is 250 kilometres (180 miles) long, while the women compete over 140 kilometres (86 miles). Near the finish line, the fastest sprinters break away from the pack and try to win the race.

The marathon is the toughest running race at the Olympics – runners must run for 42.195 kilometres (26.2 miles), often covering each mile in just under five minutes. The event has been part of the Games since 1896, although a women's marathon race was not added until 1984 after many years of campaigning by female runners to persuade the **International Olympic Committee** (IOC) to add the event to the Olympic programme. The longest race on foot is not the marathon, but the 50-kilometre race walk, which takes around three and a half hours. Walkers must keep one foot on the ground at all times and straighten their front leg as it hits the ground.

During a road race, cyclists bunch together in a 'pack' called a peloton.

Olympic insights

Rowers need between 4,000 and 6,000 calories per day when training. That's more than twice the amount most adults should eat. It can be difficult to eat this much, so endurance athletes must eat foods that are easily digestible but high in energy, such as rice and pasta.

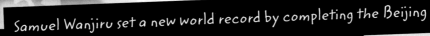

Samuel Wanjiru set a new world record by completing the Beijing Olympic marathon in two hours, six minutes and 32 seconds.

Gymnastics

The O2 was built for London's Millennium celebrations in 2000 and has since become a successful concert venue. In 2012, crowds will be thrilled by the grace and strength of the world's gymnasts as this arena hosts the Olympic gymnastic and trampolining competitions.

Olympic bounce

Trampolining is the newest sport in Olympic gymnastics, making its debut at the Sydney Games in 2000. Gymnasts perform a series of short routines, which contain a variety of twists, bounces and somersaults.

Competitors must display precise technique and perfect body control throughout their performance. Judges award points for the difficulty of the routine, the skill with which moves such as somersaults are performed and the height of the jumps achieved. Top gymnasts can reach heights of 10 metres!

Olympic insights
American George Eyser won three gold medals for gymnastics at the 1904 Olympics in St Louis, USA, which was amazing enough in itself. Even more remarkably, Eyser's left leg was made of wood. He had lost his leg after he was run over by a train.

In 2004, Anna Dogonadze of Germany won the gold medal in the women's trampolining competition in Athens.

Grace under pressure

Women's gymnastics includes combined team and individual events in four different disciplines: beam, floor exercises, uneven bars and vault. Men's gymnastics includes different disciplines, such as rings and the pommel horse, which need great upper body strength. Gymnastic competitions are marked by two panels of judges: one panel decides on the difficulty of the routine and the other marks the quality of the gymnast's performance.

Male gymnasts perform swings, handstands and strength moves (in which the body is held perfectly still) on rings elevated nine metres above the ground.

Olympics by numbers

Gymnast Larisa Latynina has won more Olympic medals than any other athlete. Between 1956 and 1964, the gymnast from Ukraine, then part of the USSR, won **18** medals including nine golds. It is possible that US swimmer Michael Phelps, who has already won **16** medals, may surpass Latynina's amazing record in 2012.

Rhythmic gymnastics, in which competitors perform floor routines using equipment such as ribbons and balls, also feature in Olympic gymnastics.

In the pool

Around 1,450 athletes will take part in the **aquatics** competitions in 2012. Each separate sport in the pool tests different skills, from the power and technique of swimming and water polo to the skill and precision of diving and synchronised swimming.

Olympic insights

Olympic swimming venues were fairly basic in times gone by. At the 1900 Paris Olympics, competitions were held in the River Seine and the pool at London's first Olympics in 1908 was in the middle of the Olympic Stadium's running track! The brand new Aquatics Centre in London's Olympic Park has come a long way since then.

Swimming

There are four main disciplines in swimming: freestyle, backstroke, breaststroke and butterfly. Swimmers compete at distances of up to 1,500 metres. The 10-kilometre marathon swim, which takes place in open water, was added to the Olympic programme at the Beijing Olympics in 2008. The women's open water event was won by Russian swimmer Larisa Ilchenko in one hour, 59 minutes and 27.7 seconds. The men's event was won by the Netherlands swimmer Maarten van der Weijden, who finished the race with a speed of one hour, 51 minutes and 51.6 seconds.

US swimmer Natalie Coughlin competed in six events at the 2008 Games, and won a medal in each! She is currently in training for the 2012 Games.

Daring divers

In the platform event, divers try to complete complex dives that include difficult moves, such as somersaults and twists. Dives are made from a diving board positioned 10 metres above the pool's surface. Judges award points for each dive, which are adjusted depending on the difficulty of the move. Points are also awarded for the diver's take-off from the diving board, the control displayed as the diver carries out the move and how 'clean' his or her entry into the water is.

Tom Daley, the British diver, hopes to win gold at the 2012 Games. At just 14 years old, he was the youngest competitor of any sport at the 2008 Olympics.

Diving together

Synchronised diving events were added to the Olympic programme in 2000. In this event two competitors from the same team perform a dive at the same time, while trying to perfectly mirror each other's movements.

" My dream is a gold... with a lot of work...I hope to achieve that. Tom Daley, speaking about his hopes for the Olympics in 2012. "

WORD FILE

Key diving terms and their meanings:

arm stand: platform dive that begins from a handstand position

pike: body position with hips bent and legs straight

springboard: event using a long board three metres above the pool

tuck: position with hips and legs bent and pulled close to the body

On the water

Most of the events on water at the 2012 Olympics will take place outside the capital. Rowing and canoe sprint events will be staged at Eton Dorney near Windsor. A specially designed **white-water** course has been built at the Lee Valley White Water Centre in Hertfordshire for canoe slalom. Sailing events will be held at Weymouth and Portland on the south coast.

Sailing at the Olympics

There will be 10 gold medals awarded for sailing at the London Olympics. Today's sailing competitions use small, light boats with no more than three people on board. Each crew member can directly affect the balance and performance of the boat, making sailing a test of the agility and skill of each athlete. Sailors must position their bodies and the boat's sails perfectly to balance the vessel and to make use of the wind.

Olympic insights

Great Britain has been the most successful sailing nation in the last three Olympics. Ben Ainslie has won gold medals at each Games since Sydney in 2000, and the British team won three gold medals in 2008.

In the laser class sailing event, each small dinghy is manned by just one sailor.

White-water winners

Canoes and kayaks used in canoe slalom are small and light to make it easier for athletes to guide them around poles, called gates, on a challenging white-water course. Athletes race against the clock and there are time penalties for touching or missing a gate. In canoe sprint races, individuals or teams of two or four paddlers race each other over distances of up to 1,000 metres on a straight course.

In the white-water canoe slalom event, athletes must navigate a 300-metre course without touching the gates.

WORD FILE

Key sailing terms and their meanings:

class: *the model of boat. Olympic sailors race against each other in the same class of boats*

dinghy: *small sailing boat*

fleet racing: *style of race used at the Olympics when all the competitors race against each other*

match racing: *style of race in which one boat races against another. Match racing will feature in the women's competition in 2012*

trapese: *harness fitted to the mast of a boat so sailors can safely put all their weight over the side of the boat*

Combat sports

Many of the **combat sports** at the Olympics have ancient origins. Boxing and wrestling were part of the ancient Games in Greece and will still feature in London in 2012. Fencing developed from **swordsmanship**, and evidence has been found that indicates sword fighting was a sport in many ancient cultures, including the gladiator swordfights in ancient Roman arenas.

Taekwondo is practised by 60 million people worldwide. Afghan Rohullah Nikpai (above left) won his country's first Olympic medal when he took the bronze in 2008.

Punching and kicking

Taekwondo means 'the art of punching and kicking' in Korean. As the name suggests, each taekwonda (athlete) tries to hit an opponent with the hands or feet. The sport developed from several ancient combat techniques going back more than 2,000 years, although the name taekwondo was only given to the sport in the 1950s.

The gentle way

Judo means 'gentle way' in Japanese. The aim of judo is to score an 'ippon', meaning 'one full point'. This can be achieved by throwing the opponent onto their back and keeping them under control by pinning them down on the floor for 30 seconds.

WORD FILE

Key judo terms and their meanings:

judogi: white or blue cotton jacket and trousers worn for judo

judoka: an expert or competitor in judo

matte: shouted by the referee to interrupt a fight. Athletes must separate when hearing this

tatami: mat that is used for a judo contest

The main principle of judo is that a competitor does not resist, but turns the opponent's force against him.

In the ring

Originally **professional** athletes were not allowed to compete at the Olympics, and while this has changed for many sports, just **amateurs** are still only allowed to compete in Olympic boxing events because its rules are very different from those of professional boxing. Like most combat sports at the Olympics, boxers are divided into different weight divisions so that athletes compete against others of a similar size. Olympic boxers win a point for each punch they land on their opponent's head or upper body. Each match is made up of four rounds lasting two minutes.

Boxing was once a male-only event at the Olympics, but in 2012 women's boxing will feature for the first time.

Team sports

Many Olympic sports rely on teamwork just as much as individual brilliance to win medals. Team athletes range from amateur hockey and handball players to high-profile football stars and basketball teams. Sports such as basketball have become popular since professionals have been allowed to compete at the Olympics, and huge crowds gather at the Games to see top players in action.

Olympic football

Men's football at the Olympics is a competition for players under the age of 23. Each team is also allowed to include three players over that age. The last two Olympic men's tournaments have been won by Argentina, with young stars including Carlos Tevez and Lionel Messi in the team. Women's football has no age limits. The USA has won three gold medals since women's football was first played at the Olympics in 1996.

Cycling teams

Both road and track cycling will be 2012 events. British stars such as Chris Hoy and Victoria Pendleton will be hoping to continue their dominance of track cycling at the London Olympics. To do this, they will have to work as teams in events including the team sprint and team pursuit, in which each cyclist in the team takes a turn leading the race to save the energy of other team members.

Football star Ronaldinho celebrates a goal against New Zealand with other members of the Brazilian team at the 2008 Games.

Horse and rider

All **equestrian** events are for teams of horses and their riders. As well as individual medals, there are medals for the best teams of three horses and riders from each nation. In the three equestrian sports of dressage, jumping and eventing both men and women compete against each other. In dressage, horses are tested on movements such as the piaffe (trotting on the spot) and the half-pass (moving forwards and sideways at the same time).

Eventing includes **dressage**, jumping (shown above) and cross-country riding.

Olympics by numbers

From 1936, when basketball first appeared at the Olympics, the USA won **62** games in a row before losing in the final in 1972. In 1992, professional NBA stars appeared at the Olympics for the first time. The US 'Dream Team' averaged **117** points per game and won all their games by more than **30** points, taking the gold medal.

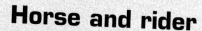

The US basketball team claimed gold once more at the 2008 Olympics and are the strong favourite to win again at the 2012 Games.

What a racket!

The Olympic tennis champions in 2012 will be crowned on Wimbledon's Centre Court. Rafael Nadal will have to work hard to defend the title he won in 2008 as stars such as Roger Federer and Andy Murray will play a tough game, knowing that the chance to be an Olympic champion only comes every four years. The Williams sisters will probably be the team to beat in the women's doubles and the 2012 Games will also feature mixed doubles for the first time since 1924.

Olympics by numbers

Racket sports players need amazingly fast reactions. A table tennis ball travels at **160** kilometres per hour. The fastest servers in tennis can send the ball across the net at more than **225** kilometres per hour. A badminton shuttlecock can travel at more than **300** kilometres per hour.

Fast and furious

Tennis is not the only Olympic racket sport. Badminton matches are fast and exciting, with players hitting the shuttlecock as hard as possible to force the opposition to make a mistake.

Doubles competitions are even quicker than singles matches because players do not have to move as far to return the shuttlecock. The shuttlecock is made of cork surrounded by 16 feathers from the left wing of a goose. It has to stay in the air at all times. Points are won if players can hit the shuttlecock onto the ground on their opponent's side of the net.

Elena Dementieva won gold at the 2008 Beijing Olympics. The Russian star player has since retired and will not make an appearance at the 2012 Games.

24

Table tennis, like badminton, is dominated by players from Asian countries including China, where it is a massively popular sport. It became an Olympic sport in 1988. The game moves very fast so it is easy to miss the techniques that top competitors use to try to outwit their opponents, such as spins and lobs.

Badminton star Lin Dan of China was overjoyed to win gold at the 2008 Games in his home country.

Olympic insights

Table tennis originated in the UK during the 1880s, where it was an after-dinner pastime in wealthy households. It has since become an international sport that is now dominated by China, the hot favourites to take home the gold in 2012.

Ryu Seung Min (top) brought victory to South Korea when he took the table tennis gold at the 2004 Games in Athens. It was the first time since 1992 that the gold medallist had not been Chinese.

Winter sports

The sports that make up the Summer Olympics are really only part of the Olympic story. Winter sports such as **figure skating** and ice hockey were included in the Summer Olympics in 1920, but then became features of the Winter Games in 1924. The next Winter Olympics will be held in Sochi, Russia, in 2014.

High-speed sports

All sports at the Winter Olympics take place on snow or ice. Sliding sports such as bobsleigh, luge and skeleton are the fastest sports at the Winter or Summer Olympics, with athletes hurtling down a sheet of ice at around 145 kilometres per hour. At 130 kilometres per hour, Olympic downhill skiers travel almost as fast.

Olympic bobsleigh teams can be made up of a four-person crew (above) or a two-person crew. Each team competes to achieve the fastest speed as they slide down a track of ice.

Olympics by numbers
The Vancouver Winter Olympics in 2010 welcomed **2,566** athletes from **82** countries. They competed in **86** events across **15** sports.

Skating stars

Figure skaters showcase dazzling routines on ice. Skaters perform to music and include challenging moves such as jumps and spins in their routines. Skaters are judged on the complexity of their moves and the skill with which they perform their routine. Speed skating is a high-speed race in which racers can reach speeds of 95 kilometres per hour.

In ice hockey, players aim to hit a rubber **puck** into the opposing team's goal. Players use shoulders and hips to tackle opponents as they try to gain control of the puck.

Speed skaters wear **aerodynamic** body suits that keep them warm while allowing them to move freely on the ice.

WORD FILE

Key Winter Olympic sports:

biathlon: *sport that combines cross-country skiing with shooting*

curling: *sport in which two teams slide 'stones' or rocks along the ice towards a target*

luge: *sliding event in which one or two athletes lie on their backs on a sled*

skeleton: *sliding event in which one athlete lies face-down on a sled and slides down a track of ice*

New sports

The Winter Olympics have also been quick to take in newer sports such as snowboarding and **freestyle skiing**. New events at the Vancouver Winter Olympics in 2010 included ski cross, in which skiers raced against each other over a twisting course with bumps and jumps. New events at the 2014 Winter Olympics in Russia will include **ski halfpipe**, **biathlon** mixed relay and a figure skating team event.

27

Changing Olympic sports

There were nine sports at the first 'modern' Olympic Games in 1896. Some sports, such as athletics, swimming and fencing, have been part of the Games ever since. Many new sports have been added and removed as the Olympic Games have become a global event, culminating in a huge variety of sports that will feature in London in 2012.

Sports can be dropped from the Olympic programme. Baseball and softball were the most recent sports to be removed after the 2008 Olympics. The IOC, which decides which sports should be part of the Games, felt that these sports did not have enough worldwide appeal.

Olympic insights

Some unusual sports were part of the Olympics in the past, such as tug-of-war, Jeu de Paume (also called **real tennis**) and motorboating. All are no longer featured in the Games. Squash, karate and roller sports (such as roller skating) failed in their bid to become Olympic sports in 2016, but golf and rugby sevens were successful and will feature at the 2016 Games in Rio de Janeiro.

Rugby sevens is played by seven members in each team. Matches are made of two halves, with each lasting 10 minutes.

Sports for everyone

The **Olympic Movement** continually reviews the many sports featured at the Olympics, and updates its programme to include new sports. BMX and mountain biking became Olympic sports in 2008. These sports developed during the 1970s and 1980s as bikes became light and tough enough to race across rough terrain.

Paralympics

Just a few weeks after the Olympics, athletes with disabilities will meet in London for the 2012 Paralympics. Athletes with disabilities will take part in 20 different sports using the same sporting venues as the Olympics. Many of these sports, such as wheelchair athletics or cycling for the **visually-impaired**, are adapted versions of Olympic sports.

Visually-impaired runners race with a sighted guide companion. The two runners hold a tie that joins them during the race.

Olympic trivia

Discover some amazing facts and figures about the Olympics.

At the first 'modern' Olympic Games in Athens in 1896, silver medals were awarded to the winners.

Athletes at the ancient Olympics in Greece competed naked.

More athletes than spectators attended the 1900 Olympics in Paris.

Women were first allowed to compete at the Olympics in the 1900 Games.

The oldest person to ever compete at the Olympics was Oscar Swahn, a Swedish shooter. He won his sixth Olympic medal at the 1920 Games in Antwerp, Belgium, when he was 72 years old!

The youngest person to ever compete at the Olympics was 10-year-old Greek gymnast Dimitrios Loundras. He competed in the 1896 Olympics in Athens.

Men and women compete against each other in only two Olympic sports – sailing and equestrian events.

Pigeon shooting was once an Olympic sport.

The medals for the 2008 Beijing Games were inlaid with a piece of jade. In Chinese culture, jade represents beauty and excellence in all things.

Between 1900–1920, the Olympics included a tug-of-war event.

The design of the Olympic flag, with five rings, was created by Pierre de Coubertin in 1914.

Glossary

aerodynamic designed to move through air with maximum speed

amateurs people who are not paid for what they do

aquatics sports that take place in water, such as swimming and diving

biathlon a sporting competition made up of two events

bobsleigh a sport in which teams of two or four people travel down an ice track in a sled-like vehicle

carbon fibre light, strong material

combat sports sports where athletes simulate combat. Many of these sports had their origins in training for soldiers

discus an event in which a metal disc is thrown as far as possible

dressage an equestrian event (see below) in which horses perform movements such as trotting on the spot

equestrian relating to horses

figure skating performing ice skating routines with moves such as jumps

freestyle skiing a form of skiing in which skiers ski down a ramp and jump into the air, where they perform acrobatic moves such as spins

hammer an event in which a heavy ball attached to a wire and handle is thrown

host to stage or organise an event

hurdlers runners that also jump over fences called hurdles during the race

International Olympic Committee the organisation that leads the Olympic Movement and oversees the organisation of the Olympic Games

javelin an event in which a spear-like object called a javelin is thrown as far as possible

Olympic Movement the name for all the groups involved in planning the Olympics

origins beginnings, such as when and where a sport was first played

Paralympics a sporting event for athletes with disabilities

professional someone who is paid for what they do

puck a small, round object that is hit into a net to score a goal

real tennis the original form of tennis (once called royal tennis) that was played by kings such as Henry VIII

shot put an event in which a heavy metal ball is thrown as far as possible

ski halfpipe an event in which skiers ski down a U-shaped ramp and perform tricks in the air at each end

sledgehammer a very large hammer with a heavy metal or wooden head

steeplechase a hurdle event in which athletes race over hurdles that include water jumps

swordsmanship skill with a sword

venues buildings or locations where something happens. Each Olympic sport takes place in a particular venue

visually-impaired a disability affecting the eyes and a person's ability to see

white-water water flowing over rocks and obstacles to create a course for canoe slalom

Further information

Books

British Olympians (21st Century Lives)
by Debbie Foy (Wayland, 2009)

Cycling (Olympic Sports)
by Clive Gifford (Franklin Watts, 2011)

High-Tech Olympics (Olympics)
by Nick Hunter (Raintree, 2011)

Improving Speed (Training for Sport)
by Paul Mason (Wayland, 2010)

Websites

Find out more about Olympic sports, athletes and records by exploring the world governing body for athletics at:
www.iaaf.org

For information about swimming and other aquatic sports, visit the world governing body for water sports at:
www.fina.org

Visit the official 2012 Olympic websites:
www.london2012.com/sports
www.olympic.org/sports

Index

badminton 24–25
basketball 5, 22, 23
BMX racing 5, 29

canoeing 18, 19
combat sports 11, 20–21, 28
cycling 4, 5, 10, 12, 13, 22, 29

discus throwing 8, 9, 11
diving 4, 16, 17

endurance sports 10–11, 12–13
equestrian sports 11, 23

football 22

gymnastics 14–15

hammer throwing 9
high jump 8, 11
hurdling 6, 7, 11

javelin throwing 8, 9, 11

kayaking 18, 19

long jump 8, 11

Paralympic sports 5, 29
pole vault 8, 11

rowing 12, 13, 18
running 4, 5, 6–7, 10, 11, 12, 13, 29

sailing 5, 18, 19
shooting 5, 11, 27
shot put throwing 8, 9, 11
swimming 5, 10, 11, 16, 28

table tennis 4, 24, 25
tennis 24, 28

volleyball 4

Winter Olympic sports 5, 10, 26–27